Serve Harder Training Program

Serve 10 to 20 mph faster in 90 days!

By

Joseph Correa

COPYRIGHT PAGE

Copyright © 2017 Joseph Correa

All rights reserved. This book or any portion thereof may not be reproduced or used in any manner without the express written permission of the publisher except for brief book quotations for reviews in the book.

Scanning, uploading, and distributing of this book via the Internet or via any other means without the express permission of the publisher and author is illegal and punishable by law.

Only purchase authorized editions of this book. Please consult with your physician before training and using this book.

ACKNOWLEDGEMENTS

This book is dedicated to all the tennis players in the world who don't give up and keep working hard every day.

Serve Harder Training Program

Serve 10 to 20 mph faster in 90 days!

By

Joseph Correa

INTRODUCTION

Serve Harder Training Program

Serve 10 to 20 mph faster in 90 days!

By Joseph Correa

Learn how to drastically change your serve through 6 exercises that will increase your racquet head speed and acceleration in a very significant way.

This book includes:

- 6 Tennis Serve exercises
- 3 charts that will teach you how to do them in an organized manner.
- Detailed explanation on each phase of the charts.
- 6 Serving tips
- 15 Serve drills

This is your chance to have the best serve ever with this training that will change the way you approach your serve. Using a scientifically proven method to increase your racquet head speed and acceleration through 6 exercises.

Do you want to win more matches thanks to your serve?

Want to make a big difference in the results you have in your matches and tournaments?

Well, in tennis, YOU SPEND AT LEAST 46% OF THE TIME SERVING! Which means that the better you serve, the better your chance you will have of controlling that 46% of your match.

The remainder of the match you spend on returning serve and hitting ground strokes and volleys during the point. This basically means that working on your forehand, backhand, over head, slice, topspin, return of serve, and other specific shots will require a lot more time and effort to master the remaining 54% of your match.

SO WHY NOT WORK ON WHAT MATTERS THE MOST?

This book will:

- change how you serve.

- It will reduce shoulder injuries.

- It will reduce the amount of running you will have to do in your matches.

- It will teach you how to serve faster than ever before
- It will save you tears, frustration, time, and most importantly losses

It includes 3 charts that explain in detail when to train, how to train, how many times to train, and what to train. Each chart is specific for "before competition training", "during competition training", and "during your off season training" which may be in the summer or during the winter time so that you can maximize results.

Make the investment in your game to change how you play and WIN MORE TROPHIES!

This book will teach you how to serve 10-20 mph faster in a 3 month period with a day by day program. The best serve training program in the market.

This book shows you how to do the exercises properly and efficiently. You will learn the process you should follow in order to be successful with the program.

ABOUT THE AUTHOR

Hello, my name is Joseph Correa and I have been training and teaching tennis for over 20 years. I played professional tennis for many years and am a USPTR professional certified coach.

After years of competing and training with some of the best players in the world I have learned that most people can be very successful in competition with the right mental, physical, and emotional training.

Proven scientific techniques, drills, and step by step phases must be performed to reach your peak and for that reason I have prepared the first group of training DVD's and books showing you how to reach your goals.

Through my work and teaching aids, I have helped hundreds of amateur and professional tennis player's advance with their physical, mental, and performance goals to achieve great results.

Best of luck,

Joseph

TABLE OF CONTENTS

COPYRIGHT PAGE

ACKNOWLEDGEMENTS

INTRODUCTION
ABOUT THE AUTHOR

TABLE OF CONTENTS

PART 1: *HOW TO PERFORM THE EXERCISES*

PART 2: *INTERPRETING THE CHARTS*

PART 3: *SIX SECRETS TO A FASTER SERVE*

15 TENNIS SERVE DRILLS TO MASTER CONSISTENCY, SPIN, AND POWER

OTHER TITLES BY JOSEPH CORREA

PART 1

HOW TO PERFORM THE EXERCISES

This is a servetraining workout that produces results and will get you serving 10 to 20 mph faster than you originally served before starting this program. Remember that there are a number of things that contribute towards having a harder serve. We will go over them one at a time. Remember to work the program so that the program works for you. In other words, follow the charts and the manual without skipping steps or days in the training calendar so that you see the best results in the least amount of time.

First of all let´s go over what you will need:

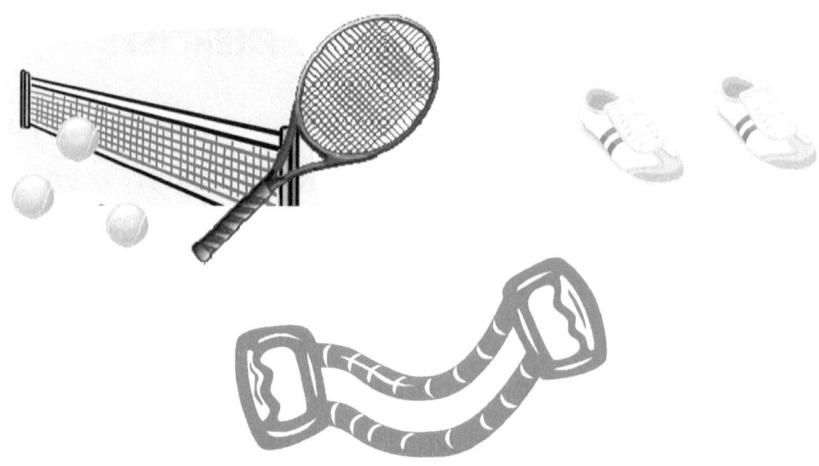

You will need:

✓ 1 TENNIS RACQUET (PREFERABLY YOURS)

✓ 10 TENNIS BALLS (ANY TYPE)

✓ 1 BOUNCEABLE MEDICINE BALL

✓ 1 STRETCHABLE OR ELASTIC EXERCISE BAND

✓ TENNIS ATTIRE (COMFORTABLE EXERCISE CLOTHES)

✓ TENNIS COURT

Serve Harder Training Program

In order to serve harder you need to have 6 basic elements that work in harmony. In this case, we are going to focus on 6 exercises performed in different sports but used in a similar way as in the tennis serve.

Having a good toss just like a juggler is *the first* and most important element. Having a good toss equals having the potential to having a good serve and having a bad toss is the equivalent to never having a good serve. It only makes sense to think, that if you will be reaching a faster serving speed than your normal, you need to make sure the ball is at the right place at the moment of impact.

The second element is **aim.** If you want to aim like an archer, proper posture is necessary. In tennis, a proper posture is obtained by holding a "tennis trophy position" before starting your acceleration. Look for a tennis trophy and copy that position. You will see a similar form to an archer but directed upwards and with a deep knee bend.

The third element is **coiling before hitting the ball**. Most quarterbacks in football have incredible throwing power and the main reason why they can generate so much acceleration is because of their coiling position. Practice turning your shoulders more sideways so that you can turn towards the ball faster using all of your upper body in a second (or as fast as you can, a fraction of a second would be ideal).

The fourth element is **jumping**. This is where most advanced tennis players get the additional speed on their serves. Basketball players are masters at creating a quick and powerful vertical leap. You should learn and apply this important factor to your serve to get the results you want even though it might take a while to learn to incorporate jumping and swinging together.

The fifth element is the **swing acceleration**. We use a baseball players throw to understand the fundamental technique behind a good throwing motion since it is very similar to a tennis players arm motion when swinging a tennis racquet and creating the necessary acceleration. By improving your throw, you will improve your swing. You will be working a lot on this in the training program so that you can throw further and further every time which will equate to a stronger serve.

The sixth and last element is to **"slam the ball down"**. As important as it is to thrust your body upwards towards the ball, you still need the other half of the equation which is creating as much force downwards with both arms and your upper body when impacting the ball while keeping your head up as to maintain eye contact.

These are the 6 serve training exercises you will be doing:

1. Tennis ball throw
2. Serve accelerations
3. Squat jumps
4. Medicine ball throws
5. Band triangle
6. Complete serves

Serve Harder Training Program

Tennis ball throws should be done with a relaxed motion just like a baseball pitchers throw. Start with your weight on your back foot and finish with your weight on your front or right foot (for a righty, for a lefty it would be backwards). Try to make sure your elbow is bent, as a straight arm throw will only injure your shoulder. Use your left arm to help you turn faster by turning it to the left as your throw. You will be implementing a similar left arm pull when you serve but it will be from a vertical angle downwards as you begin impact on the ball.

Serve accelerations are the backbone of these series of exercises so make sure to do them properly. Using serve accelerations as part of your pre-serve warm up is very effective and will reduce shoulder, elbow, and wrist injuries. Serve accelerations are service swings you perform without the use of a tennis ball, which means, you are actually swinging at the air and creating a swooshing sound when you start going faster. The friction between your racquet and the air creates a whistling sound. Prepare just like a normal serve, include your jump and follow through. Finish by stepping or landing in front of the baseline. Always finish in front of the baseline. NO JUMPING BACKWARDS! If you jump backwards you will never learn to use your body weight to increase serve velocity.

Serve Harder Training Program

Squat jumps are very simple exercises that can be done on court but its better if you do them on grass or a softer surface to minimize knee impact. Also, have comfortable shoes that will absorb as much of the impact as possible since you will be performing many jumps. Bend your knees with your legs apart and your hips and gluts downwards toward the ground without letting your knees go forward (just like sitting on a chair!). Going forward with your knees causes unnecessary strain on your knees and keeping your knees together will hurt joints and ligaments so stay away from these two things. Use your arms to propel yourself upwards as you jump in the air. When landing on the ground, bring your feet together to reduce impact every time you perform this exercise.

As you repeat the squat jumps every week you should be jumping higher off the ground and this will equate to a lot more momentum towards your arm. The additional strength in your legs will help not only improve your acceleration but also will give you a higher point of impact which will help you get more serves in.

Medicine ball throws need to be performed with a ball that is acceptable to your strength level. Do not use a medicine ball over 20 pounds as it will only make your serve slower instead of faster. Try different balls and see which one is comfortable for you. Choose one based on the amount of repetitions that you see in the training chart that you can complete with proper technique. Good form is everything. You want to strengthen the right muscles every time you exercise. You should start with the ball behind your head and elbows bent. Bend your knees and throw the ball straight down so that it bounces back up to your shoulder level. Catch the ball and repeat as many times as the chart requires.

Band triangle training is advanced and needs to be done properly to gain maximum results. Start by getting down on your right knee if you are right handed (and the opposite for left-handed players).

Next, place the band around a sturdy object such as a fence, tree, net post, or other. Take the band with your right hand (assuming you are right handed, if not, do the opposite if you are left handed.) and bend your elbow as to complete a pushing and pulling motion with your right arm just like you would when you do a serve. At the same time pull your left elbow down towards your left ribs as to feel them contract and then simply go back to the same starting position which should not have any resistance on your right or left hand, and then repeat as required by the training chart. Find a band that is right for you.

A **Complete Serve** requires you to perform as many serves as stated by the training chart. Try to push and pull with all the muscles you previously worked out in the last 5 exercises of the training program. In other words, you want to make sure you are jumping, coiling, accelerating, swinging, and pulling down towards the ball on every serve. Your objective should be to work all the pieces of your serve separately and then on the 6th exercise bring them all together as a stronger and faster serve.

All 6 exercises need to be performed in the same order and with as many repetitions as required in the work out charts. Do not alter or change the order, amount, technique, or position in which you are supposed to complete them as it might affect the results negatively.

PART 2

INTERPRETING THE CHARTS

Go over each chart and determine two things:

1. **What stage of training are you in?** <u>Competition stage</u> is when you are in the middle of competition. <u>Pre-competition</u> is when you are a few months away from competing. <u>Off season</u> is the third stage and this is when you are not competing nor in pre-competition. Each chart is for a specific stage of competition so make sure you decide where you are at since the difficulty level of each chart changes drastically.

2. **What level tennis player are you?** Beginner, Intermediate, and Advanced. Each level will affect the difficulty and repetitions for each exercise. If you find one level to be too difficult you can always move down a level and move up as your ability and strength improves.

Once you have these two things clear go to the chart and columns on the chart that best describes where you are at so that you may begin training.

Serve Harder Training Program

ALWAYS WARM UP BEFORE STARTING THE SERVE HARDER TRAINING PROGRAM!

Workout training Chart — WWW.SERVEHARDER.COM — Pre-Competition

MONTH 1

	MONDAY	TUESDAY	WEDNESDAY	THURSDAY	FRIDAY	SATURDAY	SUNDAY
3 SERIES EACH	Serve Harder Training Repetitions	Serve Harder Training Repetitions	Serve Harder Training Repetitions	Serve Harder Training Repetitions	Serve Harder Training Repetitions	Serve Harder Training Repetitions	Serve Harder Training Repetitions
	Beg Interm Adv	Beg Interm Adv	Beg Interm Adv	Beg Interm Adv	Beg Interm Adv	Beg Interm Adv	Beg Interm Adv
Ball Throws	10 12 15		10 12 15		10 12 15	TOURNAMENT OR REST	TOURNAMENT OR SERVES
Accelerations	10 12 15		10 12 15		10 12 15		
Squat Jumps	10 10 15	REST	10 10 15	REST	10 10 15		
Medicine Ball Slams	10 15 18		10 15 18		10 15 18		
Band Triangle	8 10 12		8 10 12		8 10 12		ONLY 1 SERIES
Complete Serves	10 15 20		10 15 20		10 15 20		30 60 80

MONTH 2

	MONDAY	TUESDAY	WEDNESDAY	THURSDAY	FRIDAY	SATURDAY	SUNDAY
3 SERIES EACH	Serve Harder Training Repetitions	Serve Harder Training Repetitions	Serve Harder Training Repetitions	Serve Harder Training Repetitions	Serve Harder Training Repetitions	Serve Harder Training Repetitions	Serve Harder Training Repetitions
	Beg Interm Adv	Beg Interm Adv	Beg Interm Adv	Beg Interm Adv	Beg Interm Adv	Beg Interm Adv	Beg Interm Adv
Ball Throws		12 15 20	12 15 20	12 15 20		TOURNAMENT OR REST	TOURNAMENT OR SERVES
Accelerations		15 20 25	15 20 25	15 20 25			
Squat Jumps	REST	12 15 20	12 15 20	12 15 20	REST		
Medicine Ball Slams		15 20 25	15 20 25	15 20 25			
Band Triangle		10 12 15	10 12 15	10 12 15			ONLY 1 SERIES
Complete Serves		15 20 30	15 20 30	15 20 30			40 70 110

YOU SHOULD BE SERVING ATLEAST 10 MPH FASTER. IF YOU WANT TO REACH PAST 10 MPH COMPLETE MONTH 3.

MONTH 3

	MONDAY	TUESDAY	WEDNESDAY	THURSDAY	FRIDAY	SATURDAY	SUNDAY
3 SERIES EACH	Serve Harder Training Repetitions	Serve Harder Training Repetitions	Serve Harder Training Repetitions	Serve Harder Training Repetitions	Serve Harder Training Repetitions	Serve Harder Training Repetitions	Serve Harder Training Repetitions
	Beg Interm Adv	Beg Interm Adv	Beg Interm Adv	Beg Interm Adv	Beg Interm Adv	Beg Interm Adv	Beg Interm Adv
Ball Throws	15 20 25		15 20 25		15 20 25	TOURNAMENT OR REST	TOURNAMENT OR SERVES
Accelerations	20 25 30		20 25 30		20 25 30		
Squat Jumps	15 20 30	REST	15 20 30	REST	15 20 30		
Medicine Ball Slams	20 25 30		20 25 30		20 25 30		
Band Triangle	12 15 20		12 15 20		12 15 20		ONLY 1 SERIES
Complete Serves	20 25 40		20 25 40		20 25 40		60 90 150

Plan a tournament around this week as you should be performing at your best.
Tournament

CONGRATS YOU SHOULD BE PAST 20 MPH FROM YOUR ORIGINAL SERVICE SPEED! YOU WILL BE SERVING HARDER THAN EVER BEFORE! MAKE SURE TO WARM UP BEFORE AND STRETCH AFTER TRAINING TO PREVENT INJURIES.

Workout training Chart — WWW.SERVEHARDER.COM — During Competition

MONTH 1

	MONDAY	TUESDAY	WEDNESDAY	THURSDAY	FRIDAY	SATURDAY	SUNDAY
3 SERIES EACH	Serve Harder Training Repetitions	Serve Harder Training Repetitions	Serve Harder Training Repetitions	Serve Harder Training Repetitions	Serve Harder Training Repetitions	Serve Harder Training Repetitions	Serve Harder Training Repetitions
	Beg Interm Adv	Beg Interm Adv	Beg Interm Adv	Beg Interm Adv	Beg Interm Adv	Beg Interm Adv	Beg Interm Adv
Ball Throws	6 8 10		6 8 10		6 8 10	TOURNAMENT OR REST	TOURNAMENT OR SERVES
Accelerations	10 10 10		10 10 10		10 10 10		
Squat Jumps	5 7 10	REST	5 7 10	REST	5 7 10		
Medicine Ball Slams	6 8 10		6 8 10		6 8 10		
Band Triangle	10 10 10		10 10 10		10 10 10		
Complete Serves	10 15 20		10 15 20		10 15 20		

MONTH 2

	MONDAY	TUESDAY	WEDNESDAY	THURSDAY	FRIDAY	SATURDAY	SUNDAY
3 SERIES EACH	Serve Harder Training Repetitions	Serve Harder Training Repetitions	Serve Harder Training Repetitions	Serve Harder Training Repetitions	Serve Harder Training Repetitions	Serve Harder Training Repetitions	Serve Harder Training Repetitions
	Beg Interm Adv	Beg Interm Adv	Beg Interm Adv	Beg Interm Adv	Beg Interm Adv	Beg Interm Adv	Beg Interm Adv
Ball Throws		8 10 12	8 10 12	8 10 12		TOURNAMENT OR REST	TOURNAMENT OR SERVES
Accelerations		12 12 12	12 12 12	12 12 12			
Squat Jumps	REST	7 9 12	7 9 12	7 9 12	REST		
Medicine Ball Slams		8 10 12	8 10 12	8 10 12			
Band Triangle		12 12 12	12 12 12	12 12 12			
Complete Serves		12 15 20	12 15 20	12 15 20			

YOU SHOULD BE SERVING ATLEAST 10 MPH FASTER. IF YOU WANT TO REACH PAST 10 TO 20 MPH COMPLETE MONTH 3.

MONTH 3

	MONDAY	TUESDAY	WEDNESDAY	THURSDAY	FRIDAY	SATURDAY	SUNDAY
3 SERIES EACH	Serve Harder Training Repetitions	Serve Harder Training Repetitions	Serve Harder Training Repetitions	Serve Harder Training Repetitions	Serve Harder Training Repetitions	Serve Harder Training Repetitions	Serve Harder Training Repetitions
	Beg Interm Adv	Beg Interm Adv	Beg Interm Adv	Beg Interm Adv	Beg Interm Adv	Beg Interm Adv	Beg Interm Adv
Ball Throws	10 12 14		10 12 14		10 12 14	TOURNAMENT OR REST	TOURNAMENT OR SERVES
Accelerations	14 14 14		14 14 14		14 14 14		
Squat Jumps	8 10 13	REST	8 10 13	REST	8 10 13		
Medicine Ball Slams	8 10 14		8 10 14		8 10 14		
Band Triangle	14 14 14		14 14 14		14 14 14		
Complete Serves	10 15 20		10 15 20		10 15 20		

Plan a tournament around this week as you should be performing at your best.
Tournament

CONGRATS YOU SHOULD BE PAST 20 MPH FROM YOUR ORIGINAL SERVICE SPEED! YOU WILL BE SERVING HARDER THAN EVER BEFORE! MAKE SURE TO WARM UP BEFORE AND STRETCH AFTER TRAINING TO PREVENT INJURIES.

Serve Harder Training Program

Workout training Chart — WWW.SERVEHARDER.COM — **During Off Season**

MONTH 1

3 SERIES EACH	MONDAY Serve Harder Training Repetitions			TUESDAY Serve Harder Training Repetitions			WEDNESDAY Serve Harder Training Repetitions			THURSDAY Serve Harder Training Repetitions			FRIDAY Serve Harder Training Repetitions			SATURDAY Serve Harder Training Repetitions			SUNDAY Serve Harder Training Repetitions		
	Beg.	Interm.	Adv.	Beg.	Interm.	Adv.	Beg.	Interm.	Adv.	Beg.	Interm.	Adv.	Beg.	Interm.	Adv.	Beg.	Interm.	Adv.	Beg.	Interm.	Adv.
Ball Throws	10	12	15				10	12	15				10	12	15	TOURNAMENT OR REST			TOURNAMENT OR SERVES		
Accelerations	12	15	18				12	15	18				12	15	18						
Squat Jumps	10	15	20	REST			10	15	20	REST			10	15	20						
Medicine Ball Slams	10	15	18				10	15	18				10	15	18						
Band Triangle	10	12	15				10	12	15				10	12	15				ONLY 1 SERIES		
Complete Serves	20	30	40				20	30	40				20	30	40				30	50	60

MONTH 2

3 SERIES EACH	MONDAY Serve Harder Training Repetitions			TUESDAY Serve Harder Training Repetitions			WEDNESDAY Serve Harder Training Repetitions			THURSDAY Serve Harder Training Repetitions			FRIDAY Serve Harder Training Repetitions			SATURDAY Serve Harder Training Repetitions			SUNDAY Serve Harder Training Repetitions		
	Beg.	Interm.	Adv.	Beg.	Interm.	Adv.	Beg.	Interm.	Adv.	Beg.	Interm.	Adv.	Beg.	Interm.	Adv.	Beg.	Interm.	Adv.	Beg.	Interm.	Adv.
Ball Throws				12	15	20	12	15	20	12	15	20				TOURNAMENT OR REST			TOURNAMENT OR SERVES		
Accelerations				15	20	25	15	20	25	15	20	25									
Squat Jumps	REST			15	20	25	15	20	25	15	20	25	REST								
Medicine Ball Slams				15	20	25	15	20	25	15	20	25									
Band Triangle				12	15	20	12	15	20	12	15	20							ONLY 1 SERIES		
Complete Serves				25	35	45	20	30	40	20	30	40							40	70	110

YOU SHOULD BE SERVING AT LEAST 10 MPH FASTER. IF YOU WANT TO REACH PAST 10 MPH COMPLETE MONTH 3.

MONTH 3

3 SERIES EACH	MONDAY Serve Harder Training Repetitions			TUESDAY Serve Harder Training Repetitions			WEDNESDAY Serve Harder Training Repetitions			THURSDAY Serve Harder Training Repetitions			FRIDAY Serve Harder Training Repetitions			SATURDAY Serve Harder Training Repetitions			SUNDAY Serve Harder Training Repetitions		
	Beg.	Interm.	Adv.	Beg.	Interm.	Adv.	Beg.	Interm.	Adv.	Beg.	Interm.	Adv.	Beg.	Interm.	Adv.	Beg.	Interm.	Adv.	Beg.	Interm.	Adv.
Ball Throws	13	16	21				13	16	21				13	16	21	TOURNAMENT OR REST			TOURNAMENT OR SERVES		
Accelerations	20	25	30				20	25	30				20	25	30						
Squat Jumps	20	25	35	REST			20	25	35	REST			20	25	35						
Medicine Ball Slams	20	25	30				20	25	30				20	25	30						
Band Triangle	15	18	25				15	18	25				15	18	25				ONLY 1 SERIES		
Complete Serves	35	45	60				35	45	60				35	45	60				60	90	150

Tournament — Plan a tournament around this week as you should be performing at your best.

CONGRATS YOU SHOULD BE PAST 20 MPH FROM YOUR ORIGINAL SERVICE SPEED! YOU WILL BE SERVING HARDER THAN EVER BEFORE! MAKE SURE TO WARM UP BEFORE AND STRETCH AFTER TRAINING TO PREVENT INJURIES.

THE 3 STAGES OF THE SERVE HARDER TRAINING PROGRAM

During Competition

This would be when you are competing against other tennis players and are doing additional serves during competition besides this program.

During Off- Season

This is the stage when you are not competing at all and can work as hard as you want without sacrificing match results.

Pre Competition

This is the stage when you are preparing for competition and need to be at your best. This could be 1, 2, or 3 months before an event.

Serve Harder Training Program

These are the 6 exercises you will be performing during the training. You must perform 3 series of each.

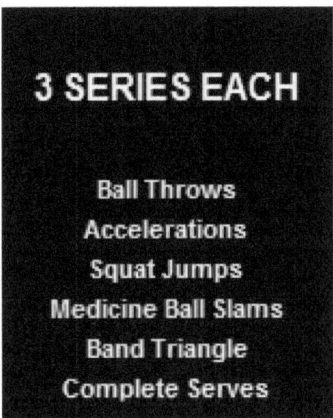

Serve Harder Training Program

This is the description of a training session for Monday on one week and the following week. The first Monday is divided into Beginner, Intermediate, and advanced. Below you will see how many repetitions you must complete depending on your level. The Monday below represents a resting day in which you do not perform any serve training.

MONDAY		
Serve Harder Training		
Repetitions		
Beg.	Interm.	Adv.
6	8	10
10	10	10
5	7	10
5	8	10
10	10	10
10	15	20

MONDAY		
Serve Harder Training		
Repetitions		
Beg.	Interm.	Adv.
	REST	

This is an example of a weekend day when you might have a tournament. In that case you would not practice serves. If, on the other hand, you do not have competition on that day, you would perform only one series of serves based on your level of play.

SUNDAY		
Serve Harder Training		
Repetitions		
Beg.	Interm.	Adv.
TOURNAMENT OR SERVES		
ONLY 1 SERIES		
30	50	80

Serve Harder Training Program

This part of the chart shows MONTH 1 and MONTH 2.

Make sure you do not skip months and follow the charts as directed.

MONTH 1 – THURSDAY
Serve Harder Training
Repetitions

Beg.	Interm.	Adv.

REST

MONTH 2 – THURSDAY
Serve Harder Training
Repetitions

Beg.	Interm.	Adv.
8	10	12
12	12	12
7	9	12
6	8	12
12	12	12
10	15	20

Serve Harder Training Program

This part in one of the charts shows an entire weeks´ training with all respective rest days. On rest days you should rest your shoulder so that you can continue working hard on the following training day.

MONTH 1

3 SERIES EACH	MONDAY Serve Harder Training Repetitions			TUESDAY Serve Harder Training Repetitions			WEDNESDAY Serve Harder Training Repetitions			THURSDAY Serve Harder Training Repetitions			FRIDAY Serve Harder Training Repetitions			SATURDAY Serve Harder Training Repetitions			SUNDAY Serve Harder Training Repetitions		
	Beg.	Interm.	Adv.	Beg.	Interm.	Adv.	Beg.	Interm.	Adv.	Beg.	Interm.	Adv.	Beg.	Interm.	Adv.	Beg.	Interm.	Adv.	Beg.	Interm.	Adv.
Ball Throws	6	8	10				6	8	10				6	8	10						
Accelerations	10	10	10				10	10	10				10	10	10	TOURNAMENT OR			TOURNAMENT OR		
Squat Jumps	5	7	10	REST			5	7	10	REST			5	7	10	REST			SERVES		
Medicine Ball Slams	5	8	10				5	8	10				5	8	10						
Band Triangle	10	10	10				10	10	10				10	10	10						
Complete Serves	10	15	20				10	15	20				10	15	20						

PART 3

SIX SECRETS TO A FASTER SERVE

SECRET # 1

Impact the Ball Out In Front of the Baseline

No serve will ever reach maximum velocity of you are hitting the ball behind you. Even though you might feel comfortable doing things the wrong way, it's still the wrong way and needs to be corrected. Old routines need to be replaced with newer and better routines. This is how you will reach your full potential. After completing a serve your whole body should have landed passed the baseline which can only mean you tossed the ball out in front of you. By throwing your body out in front of you when you serve will not only prevent injuries but will also generate much more force than just your arm by itself. Most serve injuries happen because of a bad toss, and that's usually behind your ideal point of contact.

SECRET #2

Wrist Pronation

Most people never notice one of the most important elements to a fast serve. There are two stages the ball goes through after you serve: the first is after impact, the ball goes at an initial speed upon impact in the air, and the second is the speed the ball goes after impacting the ground on your opponents' side. One of two things can happen here: either your serve hits the ground and starts to lose speed as is most common, or the ball hits the ground and maintains or increases speed. How is this possible? This is where wrist pronation comes into play. Right when you are snapping your wrist at impact with the ball you want to snap your wrist down and to the left so that your racquet face is perpendicular to the court (with your right thumb aiming down to the court, if you are a righty) instead of facing it and then bring that arm down to your opposite hip.

SECRET #3

Connect Your Feet with Your Hands

In order to generate any real power you must use your entire body. The starting point is your feet. Practice adding a stronger jump beginning with your legs. Experiment with different types of jumps, either with your feet together, apart, or coming together as you prepare for impact and see which one helps you push off the ground the hardest. The one that allows you the jump the highest or push the hardest will be the type of jump that will allow you to increase your hand speed as every serve is a chain reaction that has a beginning and an end. It all starts with your legs.

SECRET #4

Sound Biomechanics

Serve biomechanics are the basis for a good serve. It basically means how efficiently your body connects with every other part to create a smooth and effortless service motion. Having good technique on your serve is the only way you will reach serve speeds passed 100 mph. Make sure you have a good coach to go over it with you. This training program includes one-on-one coaching so make sure ask questions and get the most out of it.

SECRET #5

Keep You Head and Chin Up

By keeping your head and chin up during the service motion you promote two very important things: first you allow yourself to watch the ball longer which will allow you to impact the ball cleaner which will equal a faster serve immediately, and second, it will help you to keep your left arm up so that you can use it to pull down at the right moment and generate good body rotation. Good form is essential. Make sure you remind yourself to keep your head up by keeping your left arm up (if you are right handed and the opposite if you are left handed) as long as possible to maintain a good frame of body.

SECRET #6

Impact the Ball on the Highest Part of the Strings

Most people probably never check to see where they are impacting the ball on their strings and so miss out on the potential to add more mph's to their serve. You should always strive to hit the ball on the high part of your strings as to create the most leverage on your swing. Low contact on the strings will never generate as much acceleration as a ball that is impacted on the high part of the racquet. Check to see where most tennis ball hairs are left on your racquet and work to find the ideal point upon impact. Keep working at it until you find this spot. Also, creating a larger circle with your swing by reaching your arm out is also part of this concept of leverage so make sure you don't impact the ball with a tight or completely straight elbow. Stay relaxed and swing freely through the ball. Using leverage as a tool to increase the speed of your serve will allow you to achieve results faster.

15 SERVE DRILLS TO MASTER CONSISTENCY, SPIN, AND POWER

1. **Higher First Serve Percentage Drill**

Make sure you warm up first before hitting hard serves. First serves can be served flat, with slice, or with kick or topspin depending on what your preferred style of play is so you don't necessarily have to just hit flat and hard. Often players that play on clay use what's called a three quarters serve. This is simply a very fast second serve which is normally done with spin but taking a lot more risk on it.

Start serving on the deuce side of the court. You are going to serve and when the ball lands on the service box you are going to call that "1 first serve in a row". The next serve you hit should go in for you to call it "2 first serves in a row" but if you miss your serve you simply go back to zero. The goal is to get to the highest number of consecutive first serves in. If for any reason you are 10 or 15 serves and miss, you must go back to zero as that is how this drill is done. Once you feel you have reached the highest number possible, you will switch to the ad side of the court and do the same, Switching serving sides is very important since most people serve better off one side than the other but you can only determine this by making sure you give yourself a chance on both sides to determine your highest number possible.

This drill will help you improve your first serve percentages which will normally get more free points in your match. Remember to right done what your highest number was on each side so that you can go back and try to improve off that number the following day or week.

2. Higher Second Serve Percentage Drill

The second serve percentage drill is very simple. You're going to start on the deuce side of the court. Begin by serving a second serve and if the serve goes in count "1 second serve in a row". When you get to two serves in a row count "2 second serves in a row". If you miss a serve you must go back to zero. Your goal is to reach the highest number possible as to improve your confidence under pressure and become more consistent.

Once you're done serving on the deuce side switch to the ad side of the court and serve from there. Switching is important so that you can figure out on which side you serve better. Most people have a stronger side or a favorite side. Write down your highest number for both sides and then try to improve off that number every time you practice serves.

3. **Match Preparation Drill**

You're going to play a match against yourself and without an opponent on the other side of the court. Begin by serving two serves. A first serve and a second serve. If you get your second serve in you don't have to serve a second serve, just like in a real match. If you get your first serve in you count "15-0" and move on to the ad side as you would normally do in a real tennis match. If you miss your first serve you should serve a second serve. If the serve goes in you would count it as a point but if you miss your second serve you count that point against you as you would normally "0-15". Count just like a normal match. Once you finish the first game, move on to the second game. Your goal is to finish winning the set by reaching 6 games just like a normal match. If you win 6-0 then you should on to the next two drills described below but if you win 6-4 or lose 3-6, you should spend more time on this drill before moving on to the next two drills below.

4. Match Preparation Drill for First Serves

You're going to play a match against yourself and without an opponent on the other side of the court. Begin by serving two serves. A first serve and another first serve in replacement of a second serve. If you get your first serve in you don't have to serve a second serve, just like in a real match. If you get your first serve in you count "15-0" and move on to the ad side as you would normally do in a real tennis match. If you miss your first serve you should serve a second serve (which for this drill be another first serve). If the serve goes in you would count it as a point but if you miss your second serve you count that point against you as you would normally "0-15". Count just like a normal match. Once you finish the first game, move on to the second game. Your goal is to finish winning the set by reaching 6 games just like a normal match but by only serving first serves, even when you are supposed to serve a second serve.

This drill will greatly improve your first serve percentage under pressure and in a match.

5. Match Preparation Drill for Second Serves

You're going to play a match against yourself and without an opponent on the other side of the court. Begin by serving two serves. A second serve (instead of a first serve) and another second serve. If you get your first serve in you don't have to serve a second serve, just like in a real match. If you get your first serve in you count "15-0" and move on to the ad side as you would normally do in a real tennis match. If you miss your first serve you should serve a second serve (which for this drill will be one more serve). If the serve goes in you would count it as a point but if you miss your second serve you count that point against you as you would normally "0-15". Count just like a normal match. Once you finish the first game, move on to the second game. Your goal is to finish winning the set by reaching 6 games just like a normal match but by only serving second serves, even when you are supposed to serve a first serve.

This drill will greatly improve your second serve percentage under pressure and in a match.

6. The Side to Side Drill

For this drill you want to start by serving from the deuce side of the court. Start by serving out wide and then switch and serve down the middle or also known as the "center T". Alternate each time you hit a ball so that you never serve to the same side. Once you hit 30-100 balls on the deuce side of the court switch and do the same on the other side. The amount of serves you hit is determined by your level of play and also by how many serves you can hit without hurting your shoulder, especially if you have had shoulder problems in the past.

7. The 3-in-1 Serve Drill

For this drill you want to start by serving from the deuce side of the court. You will serve to the three common spots in the service box: out wide, to the body, and down the middle or center "T". Begin by serving out wide first, then make your next serve go to your opponents body, and the last or third ball you serve should go down the middle or center of the court. You're going to repeat the pattern every time to improve your aim.

Once you hit 30-100 balls on the deuce side of the court switch and do the same on the other side. The amount of serves you hit is determined by your level of play and also by how many serves you can hit without hurting your shoulder, especially if you have had shoulder problems in the past.

8. The Going Forward Serve Drill

Start by placing a cone about 4-6 feet from the service line in front of where ever you decide to stand when you serve. You will need to serve and then run forward towards the cone and run around it in a counter-clockwise motion and always facing the other side of the court so you never run turning around. When you return back to the service line, take another ball and do it again. The goal is to start making contact more out in front and past the service line as to benefit from being closer to your target which will always be the service box on the opposite side of the court. This drill will help you do many positive things for your serve:

1. It will improve your toss.

2. It will help you to fully reach forward when making contact so that your arm isn't restricted or tucked in when hitting the ball.

3. The drill will teach you to use your whole body not just your arm to generate power.

4. It will also improve your net game as you will be constantly moving towards the net.

5. You will learn to hit down into the court and not upwards to the other side of the court.

6. Your chin will remain up longer than usual which will get you more balls over the net.

Once you hit 30-100 balls on the deuce side of the court switch and do the same on the other side. The amount of serves you hit is determined by your level of play and also by how many serves you can hit without hurting your shoulder, especially if you have had shoulder problems in the past.

9. Serve and Volley Drill

For the serve and volley drill you need to start on the service line. Start by serving and moving forward towards the net. You will need to complete an imaginary volley on the forehand side. I like to call this a simulated volley since you are not going to make contact with any ball on that shot but you will need to use your best technique and effort on it so that you don't just rush through it. The key is to make sure you cross the mid court line before you volley so that you have gone all the way to the net. This is a very physically demanding drill but is worth the effort.

Do this 10-50 times on the deuce side of the court and splitting the serves between half forehand volleys and half backhand volleys when you come into the net. You can add an overhead after the volley which will even further improve your serve and volley game. Total serves would be 30-100 serves on the deuce side.

Once you hit 30-100 balls on the deuce side of the court switch and do the same on the other side. The amount of serves you hit is determined by your level of play and also by how many serves you can hit without hurting your shoulder, especially if you have had shoulder problems in the past.

10. The Three-Quarters Serve Drill

For the three-quarters serve drill you want to stand on the service line on the deuce side of the court. You will need to serve a fast second serve as to still have some form of control and consistency over the serve but be a lot more aggressive with it. It should be a serve that gives your opponent trouble to return but should not necessarily be an ace. The best way to do this is with a slice or kick serve but can still be done just flat if you don't have any spin serves.

Once you hit 30-100 balls on the deuce side of the court switch and do the same on the other side. The amount of serves you hit is determined by your level of play and also by how many serves you can hit without hurting your shoulder, especially if you have had shoulder problems in the past.

11. The "Move-Around the Baseline" Serve Drill

For this drill you will need to stand on the deuce side of the service line and start as close to the middle as possible. You will serve from that spot and then take step to the right and serve again. You will repeat this until you get to the doubles alley. At that moment you will begin serving by taking a step to the left as to move back to the middle of the court. Do not rush when doing this drill. Complete a serve and then step to the side and complete the next serve so that you get used to serving from different angles on the baseline.

Once you hit 30-100 balls on the deuce side of the court switch and do the same on the other side. The amount of serves you hit is determined by your level of play and also by how many serves you can hit without feeling fatigued.

12. The Variety Serve Drill

For this drill you will need to know how to serve flat, with slice, and with topspin or kick serve in order to perform it. For this drill you will begin by standing on the deuce side of the court and you will start serving a flat serve followed by a slice serve followed by a topspin or kick serve. This order is important but not strict since you can go from a flat serve to a kick serve without a problem and then to a slice serve. The key here is variety. You are not allowed to serve the same serve in a row. You must mix each serve after hitting the last one. This will help you win many more serves and have more service winners because of the difficulty level it will give your opponent. Mixing serves will benefit you more than just being predictable.

Once you hit 30-100 balls on the deuce side of the court switch and do the same on the other side. The amount of serves you hit is determined by your level of play and also by how many serves you can hit without hurting your shoulder, especially if you have had shoulder problems in the past.

Serve flat, slice, top spin serves in that order for 30 balls in a row.

13. Power Serve Training Drill

For this drill you want to start by serving from the deuce side of the court. You will begin by serving soft in order to slow bring up the serve speed every time you serve a ball. The first serve you hit should go very slow, the second should go a little faster, etc. When you get to your sixth serve hit, having started soft on serve 1, you should be hitting your hardest. Repeat this process three times going from slow to fast as to warm up you serve and to figure out what you hardest or fastest serve is. Once you know just how hard you can serve you will only serve hard until you hit 20-60 balls on the deuce side of the court switch and do the same on the other side. The amount of serves you hit is determined by your level of play and also by how many serves you can hit without hurting your shoulder, especially if you have had shoulder problems in the past.

Make sure for this drill that you still try to maintain as good technique as possible so that you're now just going for power and losing what's most important for your serve, which is smoothness. Having a smooth and relaxed serve will get you a much faster serve and doing it with proper technique will make it much more possible to do it effectively.

14. The Short Court Serve Drill

For this drill you want to start by serving from the deuce side of the court but now you will stand on the mid-court line. Your goal is to serve into the service box as you normally would but now you will be standing much closer inside the court. You are allowed to toss the ball and make contact as out in front of you as you want without foot-faulting. Complete 20 serves from both the deuce and ad sides. Write down how many of your serves landed in and if the second bounce hit the back fence or if it did not reach the back fence. For advanced players, measure just how high on the back fence you hit and work on getting it to reach higher every time.

After completing 20 serves on each side while standing right before the mid-court line, take a step back and serve a ball into the service box. Next, take another step back and serve again. Slowly continue taking a step back every time you finish serving until you reach the baseline which is where you will stay once reaching that spot on the court. When you reach the baseline serve 20 more serves from there on both the deuce and ad sides of the court. Once you reach the baseline remember to aim higher on your serve since your serves might tend to go to the net at first because of the angle at which your racquet got used to hitting at when you were at the mid-court line.

15. The On-Your-Knees Serve Drill

For this drill you will need a comfortable mat or towel that will not give your knees any pain if you kneel on it. Begin by kneeling on the mat while being right on the baseline on the deuce side of the court. Take a ball and serve into the service box. You will complete a normal serve except the lower half of your body will be eliminated since you will be on your knees. Complete 10-20 serves while on your knees, then stand up and do 10-20 normal serves without the mat. This is your first round of serves. Go back down on your knees and begin the second round of serves. The combination should be a round of serves on your knees followed by a round of normal standing serves. Repeat this process 3 times to complete one side of the court. You should have served 30-60 serves on the deuce side by the time you are done. Once you are done with the deuce side move the mat to the ad side and start the process all over again. By the end of this drill you should have completed 60-120 serves. The amount of serves will depend on you comfort level and just how hard you decide to work that day.

CAUTION: Do not complete all the drills above on the same day as you are not supposed to do 1,000 serves in a day or training session. Choose one or two at a maximum for a day or training session and work on those. All of these drill are great and will improve your serve simply choose the ones that you want to do and spread them out during the week or month to get the most out of these 15 drills. Make sure you have someone take a look at your overall technique since that is most important in having a successful serve and will help you reach your potential faster. Stretch and warm up before starting to serve. Jumping rope, jogging, doing ball throws, and doing arm circles are all good ways to warm up before serving.

OTHER TITLES BY JOSEPH CORREA

Tennis Serve Harder Training Program
by Joseph Correa

This DVD will teach you how to serve 10-20 mph faster in a 3 month day by day program. The best serve training program in the market. Video includes a 3 month chart training program and a step by step manual. The DVD shows you how to do the exercises properly and the process you should follow in order to be successful with the program.

The 33 Laws of Tennis
by Joseph Correa

The 33 Laws of Tennis is book full of valuable tennis concepts to help you become a better and more prepared tennis player. This book was written by a professional tennis player and coach in the USA. It's a very useful book that will come in handy when you least expect it and will remind you of many little but important things before competing.

Tennis Footwork and Cardio
by Joseph Correa

Joseph Correa is a professional tennis player and coach that has competed and taught all over the world in ITF and ATP tournaments for many years. Besides being a professional tennis player he has a USPTR professional coaching certification and ITF kids coaching certification.

Get in better shape and improve your mobility on and off the tennis court. Your foot work will improve drastically as well as strengthen your core and upper body. This is definitely worthwhile for a serious tennis player no matter what your level. You become faster, stronger, and more agile on the court as well as seeing an increase in acceleration in your groundstrokes and serve. Created by a professional tennis player for others to advance in their game and win more matches.

Yoga Tennis
by Joseph Correa

Yoga Tennis by Joseph Correa is a great way to improve your flexibility and agility on the court. Reach more balls and have fewer injuries. It's a great way to win more by working on a different part of your game. The DVD lasts about 30 minutes. Used by amateur and professional tennis players to improve their game and last longer in matches. This is the best way for a tennis player to become more flexible and get rid of common back, knee, shoulder, hamstring, calf, and quadriceps injuries. You´ll be glad to get started!

Tennis Abs
by Joseph Correa

Tennis Abs is a great way to strengthen your core for more powerful serves, forehands and backhands as well as stronger volleys. Abdominals are fundamental for a better game. This DVD works on many types of crunches, sit-ups, and lateral abs and back exercises that you won´t find in other abdominal videos. Feel confident when changing your shirt during your match and hit the ball harder!

www.ingramcontent.com/pod-product-compliance
Lightning Source LLC
Chambersburg PA
CBHW060506080526
44584CB00015B/1568